THE MAJESTY OF
ST. FRANCISVILLE

Photography by Kerri McCaffety
Text by Lee Malone

PELICAN PUBLISHING COMPANY
Gretna 2014

First edition, 1989
Second edition, 2014

ISBN: 9781455618460
E-book: 9781455618477

Photo on p. 2: In a corner of the formal living room at Propinquity, a rare oil painting by Murrell Butler depicts a blue heron. Antique Colt pistols belonged to Lea Reid Williams' grandfather, a bootlegger.
Photo on p. 6: Spiraling from the ground floor to the upper levels of Ellerslie, the staircase is an engineering marvel.
Photo on p. 8: The mahogany punkah above the table and chairs at Oakley was moved back and forth to fan the diners.
Photo on p. 10: An elaborate etagere stands in the upstairs hall at Milbank, displaying antique china, figurines, and an unusual clock.

Book design by Dana Bilbray

Printed in China
Published by Pelican Publishing Company, Inc.
1000 Burmaster Street, Gretna, Louisiana 70053

To the plantation home owners and curators
who welcomed us and shared the joy
that dwells within these beautiful old homes.

Acknowledgments

Michael M. Pilie, for his perceptive encouragement.
Carl L. LeBoeuf II, laboratory technician, for his printing expertise and dedication throughout the compiling of this book.
David Floyd, site manager, Louisiana State Department of Parks, for his assistance and enthusiasm.
Mary Ellen Young of the West Feliciana Historical Society, for her assistance in gathering information on several of the plantations.
Jim Calhoun, Dr. Milburn Calhoun, Nancy Calhoun, and their staff, for their proficiency and guidance.

Contents

Introduction

In the early 1700s a group of French settlers were attracted to the long ridge located in the center of what is today West Feliciana Parish. The settlement they founded was called the Village of St. Francis in honor of St. Francis of Assisi, founder of the Franciscan Order. As the town grew, it became known as St. Francisville.

The area surrounding St. Francisville consists of East and West Feliciana parishes. These are the most verdantly beautiful parishes in Louisiana, partially because the soil was enriched for centuries by fine-grained, fertile loam deposited by transcontinental winds from glacial deposits and river deltas to the banks of the Mississippi River. Lush shrubbery and colorful blooms abound there in all seasons of the year, and countless birds nest in the trees of the fragrant woodlands.

Picturesque bayous, small rivers, and streams are interspersed throughout the Felicianas, and along the banks of the waterways vast, productive plantations were established. As the plantations prospered, grand homes were built by the owners, who became widely known for their elaborate showplaces and enchanting gardens.

For many years before the Civil War, the planters and their families enjoyed prosperity. They visited each other's homes for elegant dinner parties at which fine cuisine, including tropical fruits, were served. They also attended horse racing, which was the most exciting sport. A racing season took place at St. Francisville as early as March 1, 1831. Trips to New Orleans and to other parts of the world provided further pleasant diversion.

All of this came to an abrupt halt with the outbreak of the Civil War. Many of the planters immediately joined the Confederate Army. Their families, so unfamiliar with adversity, assumed the responsibility of managing plantation affairs. Many families rose to the challenge and faced with courage the burning of their homes, the confiscation of their food and crops, and numerous other indignities inflicted by Federal troops.

When the Civil War ended, the Confederate forces returned home to find bleak devastation. Many of the glorious mansions had been destroyed by fire, and many of them had been severely damaged. During the years of Reconstruction, the scorched earth and the lack of money caused some of the once-prosperous plantations to be abandoned. The homes that were left to the elements further deteriorated.

Numerous fortunes had been rebuilt by the 1940s and 1950s. Restoration of the timeworn homes began about that time, and many of those residences now stand proudly in their original glory. Thus, the majesty of the Felicianas has returned in all its splendor.

THE MAJESTY OF
ST. FRANCISVILLE

Between the rows of hedges, Red Diplomat, Smiling Queen, and Maureen tulips are underplanted with mixed pansies.

White tulips, begonias, and blue pansies add to the beauty of Afton Villa Gardens.

Afton Villa Gardens
St. Francisville

Afton Villa began with the Barrows and was owned and loved throughout the years by a succession of families, all of whom contributed to its strange, haunting beauty.

In 1790 Bartholomew Barrow bought the large tract of land, part of a Spanish land grant on which an early-type, eight-room house stood. After Bartholomew's death, his son David lived there with his bride, Sarah, until she died in childbirth in 1846.

A year later, David married Susan Woolfolk of Kentucky, and it was she who desired a more pretentious dwelling. Construction of the larger Afton Villa began in 1849 and lasted for eight years. David had given his wife one restriction: that the original house, for sentimental reasons, would remain intact. The new mansion therefore was built around the small cottage.

A French architect was commissioned to come to St. Francisville to supervise the work. When completed, Afton Villa was a magnificent forty-room manor of French-Gothic architecture.

After David's death, the villa changed ownership several times until it was purchased in 1945 by Mr. and Mrs. Wallace Percy. The Percys restored the house to its original splendor, only to see it destroyed by fire in 1963.

Today the gardens are open to visitors and beautifully maintained by owner Genevieve Trimble.

The gardens of Afton Villa were planned originally by a French landscape gardener. To the left of the ruins of the house are stone steps leading into a delightful formal boxwood garden, laid out as an intricate maze. Colorful camellias, sweet olive, fuscata, azaleas, and flowering bulbs bloom there profusely. Immediately below the formal garden is a large sweep of seven graded terraces that descend to the ravine. Each terrace is ablaze with vivid flowers.

Another interesting, though hidden, feature of the gardens is the network of French drains which underlies the surface of the park. The system, constructed of brick, still functions, thus preventing erosion of the rolling slopes.

In the garden behind the Afton Villa ruins are Golden Oxford tulips and Louisiana phlox underplanted with yellow pansies.

Impressive statues guard the entrance to the main gardens at Afton Villa. Note the Golden Oxford tulips.

The statue seems to be contemplating the serenity of the scene at Afton Villa Gardens created by moss-draped live oak trees.

Art and nature blends on the grounds of Afton Villa Gardens.

Near the entrance to Afton Villa Gardens is a pond with a tiered fountain.

Crystal gilt candelabras on the marble mantle in the Camilla Leake Barrow dining room.

An antique bed of simple but elegant design stands in this Barrow House bedroom. The armoire has pierced carving on top and two mirrored doors.

Camilla Leake Barrow House
St. Francisville

On historic tree-shaded Royal Street in the town of St. Francisville, Camilla Leake Barrow House stands with quiet dignity. It was built in 1809 by the town jailer, Daniel J. Manire, as a "salt box" structure consisting of two rooms on each of the two levels.

The home changed hands several times before 1858 when J. Hunter Collins bought the quaint cottage. He also bought a small cottage on an adjoining lot and had it moved so that it could be attached to the original structure of Barrow House. He then added beautiful cast-ironwork railings to the upper and lower galleries, giving the house its present stately appearance.

In 1866 W. W. Leake purchased the property, and it remained in his family's possession for 125 years. In 1895, Leake's daughter, Camilla, inherited the house and then married Dr. A. F. Barrow of Highland Plantation. Since that time it has been known as the Camilla Leake Barrow House.

Lyle and Shirley Dittloff began a new era by purchasing the beautiful old home in 1984. It is listed in the National Register of Historic Places.

This Barrow House bedroom view shows the beautiful satin lining of the full-tester bed.

The mahogany punkah shown here was moved back and forth by servants for the comfort of the diners. The mahogany Empire table and chairs, ca. 1850, and the old crystal candelabra add to the attractiveness of the room.

18

Brame-Bennett House
Clinton

A classic example of Greek Revival architecture, Brame-Bennett House was built in 1840 by David Davis, a physician and planter. The house changed hands a number of times until 1887 when the Brame family came into possession.

Letitia Brame, daughter of Judge Franklin Brame, married William H. Bennett. The house was owned by the Brame-Bennett families for five generations.

Six Doric columns support the elaborately carved entablature. The pediment contains an unusual sliding fan-shaped window. Another interesting feature of the exterior is the ornamentation above the doorways and windows.

In 1941 the house was the only residence in East Feliciana Parish chosen for a permanent graphic record in the Library of Congress by the Historic American Buildings Survey. The National Register of Historic Places in 1970 added Brame-Bennett House to its list.

Butler Greenwood
St. Francisville

Like many of the earliest settlers in the Feliciana parishes, Samuel Flower was an Anglo-Saxon who came from the East Coast soon after the American Revolution. Flower came to the area from Pennsylvania in 1770 and within a decade purchased the land where he would build Greenwood.

In 1810 a fire destroyed the original Greenwood, but Flower built a larger house on the site, which is the present Butler Greenwood Plantation home. Flower died in 1813, and the title of the plantation passed to his daughter, Harriet, who married Judge George Mathews in 1809. Mathews had an important position in the early history of the state and was appointed one of three judges of the new Louisiana Supreme Court upon its creation in 1813.

By 1860, Harriet and her son, Charles, were managing 1,400 acres of cotton and indigo crops worked by almost one hundred African slaves living in eighteen cottages. According to the US National Park Service, the history of Butler-Greenwood provides an excellent illustration of how Southern women managed great Southern plantations. After Harriet's death in 1873, the management of the estate passed to Charles's wife, Penelope.

The cottage-style plantation house has remained in the same family for eight generations. Today, fifty acres of landscaped grounds surround the house at Butler Greenwood, shaded by hundreds of live oaks planted from acorns in the 1790s. The house and gardens exhibit strong evidence of the Felicianas' English traditions and culture. Eighth-generation owner Anne Butler greets visitors and oversees bed and breakfast cottages on the grounds.

The 1850s Victorian summerhouse is a feature of Butler Greenwood Plantation's formal gardens, which are filled with heirloom plants—more than 150 camellias, azaleas, magnolia, fuscata, and sweet olive grown to immense size.

The Victorian formal parlor at Butler Greenwood Plantation is one of the area's finest and most complete, with a twelve-piece set of rosewood furniture still in the original upholstery, original tasseled lambrequins at floor-to-ceiling windows and rare calla lily drapery tiebacks, floral Brussels carpet with central medallion, rosewood Meeks étagère, all installed in the late 1850s and still in original condition. There are also portraits of family members and clothing from the late 1700s and early 1800s on display in the room.

Mahogany furnishings in the dining room where members of the same family have gathered for nine generations.

A detail from a bedroom at Butler Greenwood.

The library at Butler Greenwood is filled with rare antique documents and books.

The boxwood parterres of the antebellum formal gardens and the sunken gardens along the entrance drive are filled with camellias and azaleas of staggering size, as well as sweet olive, magnolia fuscata, and other nineteenth-century plantings. Like many great gardens of the time, the gardens of Butler Greenwood were so thoughtfully planned that there is nearly always something blooming. Cast-iron urns and benches date from the 1850s.

Catalpa
St. Francisville

After a fire destroyed the original home on the site, William J. Fort and his wife, Sally Bowman Fort, built Catalpa in 1835. Sally was the daughter of Sarah Turnbull of Rosedown and James Pirrie Bowman of Oakley.

Much of Catalpa's furnishings were originally made or purchased for the elaborate Rosedown mansion. Exquisite miniatures of Turnbull and Bowman's ancestors, a copy of John James Audubon's portrait of Eliza Pirrie, beautiful antiques, china, porcelain, and silver are found in the house.

Wide, brick steps lead to the front gallery, which is encircled by a wooden railing. Six slender colonnettes support a hipped roof. An unusual double-dormer window adds charm to Catalpa's exterior.

Live oak trees, planted as early as 1814, surround the quaint, Victorian cottage. A profusion of shrubs and flowers adds to the beauty of the gardens. Many parties were held on an island in the center of a picturesque pond. It was in this pond that many priceless treasures were hidden during the Civil War.

The strong sense of continuity and reverence for the past at Catalpa is rarely equaled, for the home remains to this day lived in and loved by descendants of the same family.

Top left: This view of Catalpa's dining room shows the heavy mahogany table, built about 1840. In the corner is a petticoat table with a marble top. Against the wall stands a mahogany etagere.

Top right: Prudent Mallard made the dining room furniture at Catalpa. On the mantel are Baccarat crystal candelabras.

Below: Moss-draped oaks and azaleas line the approach to Catalpa.

Prudent Mallard, the distinguished cabinetmaker, fashioned this elegant rosewood parlor set at Catalpa. Delicate French bisque figurines stand on the carved mantelpiece under a painting of an ancestor.

The Mallard rosewood bed at Catalpa.

The parlor features this portrait of Sarah Turnbull, daughter of Daniel and Martha Turnbull, who built Rosedown. Sarah Turnbull is the ancestor of the home's current owner, Mary Thompson.

The baby carriage, next to the gentlemen's armoire, is reputed to be the first in the South. An Old Paris washbowl and pitcher on the washstand fascinate the visitor to Catalpa.

Centenary College
Jackson

Originally opened in 1826 as the College of Louisiana, the school occupied old buildings in the town of Jackson until two dormitories were built on the present property, the east wing in 1832 and the west wing in 1837.

Because of the declining enrollment, the College of Louisiana closed after less than twenty years. It was then merged with Centenary College of Brandon Springs, Mississippi, and was renamed Centenary College of Louisiana. The main academic building was constructed between the two dormitories.

The Civil War had a profound effect on Centenary College. The institution closed for the duration of the war, and its buildings were used alternately by the Confederate and Union troops. The dormitories served as a hospital during the siege of Port Hudson in 1863, and Union troops used the main academic building as headquarters.

The college reopened after the war, but with needed repairs and low enrollment, it was unable to regain its former prosperity. In 1908, seeking a wider student population base, it was moved to Shreveport where it remains today. The main academic building and the east wing were demolished in the 1930s, and only the west wing and a professor's house still stand.

In 1979 the Centenary State Commemorative Area was added to the National Register of Historic Places.

This former professor's home on the Centenary campus is now a visitors' welcome area.

Clinton Courthouse
Clinton

Clinton Courthouse, one of the architectural treasures of Louisiana, was constructed in 1840 and is still in daily use. The present building replaced a wooden courthouse built in 1825 and destroyed by fire just four years later.

Clinton Lawyers' Row
Clinton

Constructed ca. 1840-65, this is an outstanding group of early-nineteenth-century classical-style offices. Early occupants were noted for their contributions to the political and judicial history of the area and the state.

The Cottage
St. Francisville

On a high bluff in the rolling hills near St. Francisville, the Cottage was built in 1795 by John Allen and Patrick Holland on land granted to them by Spain. The architecture and furnishings clearly indicate Spanish as well as English influence. Purchased in 1811 by Judge Thomas Butler, a well-known jurist and planter, the home was occupied and preserved by the Butler family for the century and a half before J. E. Brown bought it in 1951.

The Cottage had its most famous visitor in 1815 when Gen. Andrew Jackson and his staff stayed there en route north after the Battle of New Orleans.

Beautiful antiques, mostly in Queen Anne style, fill the interior of the house, which differs from later plantation homes. It obviously was intended to be the hub of activity on a working plantation. Many old buildings remain today: the judge's law office, the kitchen, the milk house, the saddle room, and the stable.

Slender columns span the front gallery and support a high-pitched, gabled roof. The enclosed staircase was originally built outside of the house because indoor stairways were heavily taxed by the Spanish crown.

A productive plantation for nearly two hundred years, the Cottage today is owned and operated by the heirs of Mr. and Mrs. J. E. Brown of Glencoe, Illinois.

Against this parlor window at the Cottage stands an old organ with foot pedals.

The furniture in the parlor at the Cottage dates from 1836. Made by Hoadley, the Sheraton-style grandfather clock was crafted from cherry wood and inlaid with contrasting woods. The antique etagere displays old china on its shelves.

An ornate, oval mirror hangs above the black Adams mantelpiece, which is flanked by a china cabinet and an etagere. The old-fashioned wallpaper lends charm to the dining room at the Cottage.

At the northeast end of the Cottage is the bedroom that had been used by Miss Louise Butler, the last member of the Butler family to occupy the house. The antique canopied bed has a prayer bench in front of it and a pot de chambre on the side. Old dolls and children's toys add to the atmosphere of the room.

33

Ellerslie

Near Bains

On a high bluff in the Tunica hills, judge William C. Wade built Ellerslie in 1835. He had come to the Felicianas from the Carolinas in 1830 and had married Olivia Ruffin Lane, a granddaughter of the remarkable pioneer, Olivia Ruffin Barrow.

Following Judge Wade's ownership, the splendid home was occupied by the Percy family, relatives of the Percy daughters who attended Beech Wood school, at which Lucy Bakewell Audubon, wife of noted naturalist John James Audubon, taught for many years.

A gracefully curving mahogany staircase, seemingly unsupported, rises from the hall to the upper levels. Both lower and upper floors feature a wide hall in the center with large rooms on either side.

Ellerslie ranks as one of the most nearly perfect examples of Greek Revival construction. Massive, plastered-brick Doric columns support the heavy entablature. Wide galleries and a glass-enclosed observatory add to the beauty of the exterior.

Owned by descendants of Edward Percy, Ellerslie today stands elegantly beneath age-old oaks. It presents a breathtaking view in spring when the azalea and camellia plants are in bloom, while the mighty oaks, draped in Spanish moss, give the feeling that one has returned to a bygone era.

Colorful stained glass pocket doors at Ellerslie have survived for many generations.

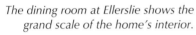

The dining room at Ellerslie shows the grand scale of the home's interior.

Ellerslie's huge windows allow fresh air to flow throughout the house. The etching above the mantle in the parlor was given to Edward Percy by New Orleans hotelier Antonio Monteleone.

Glencoe
Near Jackson

When the original Glencoe was built in 1870, it was the home of Robert Emerson Thompson and his wife, Martha Emily Scott Thompson. Martha had inherited the property from her father, Gustavus Adolphus Scott, who had purchased the land and named it Glencoe after his grandfather's hometown in Scotland.

Robert and Martha Thompson had six daughters and one son. In 1898 the family attended a party at nearby Oakland plantation in Gurley. Upon returning they found their beautiful home, which had been shingled with cedar shakes, destroyed by fire. Thompson turned to his weeping wife and said, "Don't cry, Millie. I'll build another one, but this time I'll shingle it with silver dollars." That explains the silver shingles, made of galvanized aluminum, on the present Glencoe, which was completed in 1903.

Until the arrival of the boll weevil, Glencoe was a productive cotton plantation. As his fortunes changed, Thompson decided to raise livestock, and the plantation became a cattle ranch. It is said that he was the first person in America to import an entire herd of Brahman cattle. Thirty-two were purchased in India by Thompson, but only eight survived the quarantine in New York City. The current owners are Charles Ray Morris and Leah Ann Clark Morris, who enjoy the fanciful home with their children.

Described as the finest example of Victorian-Gothic architecture in Louisiana, Glencoe was listed in the National Register of Historic Places in 1980.

Elaborate detail of Glencoe's second-floor gallery.

Through the archway of the bedroom at Glencoe one can see into the adjoining sitting room, which is located in one of the Victorian turrets.

Next page: Ornate and fanciful woodwork continues in the entry hall of Glencoe.

Greenwood
Near St. Francisville

Built in 1830 by William Ruffin Barrow and his wife, Olivia Ruffin Barrow, Greenwood plantation home was destroyed by fire in 1960. The twenty-eight plastered-brick columns, broken fireplaces, and a mass of smoldering ashes were all that remained of the grand Greek Revival mansion.

In April of 1968, Walton J. Barnes, father of the present owner, purchased the property and determined to restore Greenwood to its former glory. Photographs of the original home were used to provide detail for rebuilding the moldings, gallery railings, and decor. A fascinating old inventory book describing the interior furnishings for each room was found and helped guide the restoration.

The location of load-bearing walls, the ceiling heights, and the floor dimensions were determined from the ruins by Michael Rollinger, who drew the blueprints for the replica of the historic plantation home.

During the summer of 1968 the Barnes family cleared the site of trees, vines, and weeds. Through the winter of 1968 and into the spring of 1969, Richard Barnes continued the process of site preparation, including the task of digging out and hauling away nearly three feet of ashes and hundreds of pounds of brickwork from the ruined chimneys.

In the following years the actual restoration took place. Each of the twenty-eight columns was restored, using the original bricks, and each was given a new concrete foundation. The Barneses further improved the grounds by trimming stately oaks and landscaping the gardens. Before proceeding to the building of the mansion, the access roads also were graded.

By 1983 Greenwood had been restored to its former grandeur. The same year International Cinema Corporation contracted to use the plantation as the setting for the film *Louisiana*. Thus, with dedication, hard work, and the

assistance of family, friends, and the movie industry, Richard Barnes and his family have realized a dream. Once again, Greenwood is a magnificent Greek Revival plantation home.

This elegant, curving stairway graces the hallway at Greenwood. The magnificent archway has a pilaster and a column on each side.

Pocket doors separate the grand-scale dining room and Ladies Parlor at Greenwood.

Above the mantelpiece in the ladies' parlor at Greenwood hangs a beveled French mirror. An antique parlor set adds to the quiet beauty of the room. Through the archway the dining room seems to invite entry.

On the east wall of the gentlemen's parlor at Greenwood, the portraits of William Ruffin Barrow and his wife, Olivia Ruffin Barrow, are displayed.

An 1850 Fischer square grand piano in the Ladies' Parlor at Greenwood. Music was an integral part of plantation entertainment.

On the second floor of Greenwood are large bedrooms with grand canopy beds.

Highland
North of Bains

A winding road, lined with lush shrubbery, colorful flowers, and century-old oak trees, leads to Highland plantation house, built by William Barrow III in 1804 on a land grant from the Spanish crown.

The home was originally called Locust Ridge and was later renamed by Barrow's son, Bennett, who introduced to the area a long staple cotton which he called "Highland." After his father's death, Bennett H. Barrow enlarged the house and planted eighty-nine live oak trees during the 1830s. He also added a race track and a sugar mill. A dance hall and a hospital were built for his slaves. His diary, a fascinating commentary on life at Highland from 1836 to 1846, reflects the planter's life and views.

Mr. and Mrs. Donald Norwood, the present owners, restored the house in 1999. At the time of the restoration some of the basic timbers showed deterioration. To make the necessary replacements, Norwood tore down what was left of the old slave cabins, which were built of virgin cypress, to use in the restoration process. The handmade bricks used in the foundation, where replacements were necessary, came from the slave cabin chimneys and the racing stables which were located near the house.

Donald Norwood is the great-great-great-grandson of the original builder. Seven generations of the same family have occupied the home.

Highland has been placed on the National Register of Historic Places.

Victorian furniture in Highland's entrance hallway.

The magnificent full-tester bed made in 1854 for Highland has been extended to accommodate a king size mattress.

Right: The dining room at Highland.

Below: Portraits of Bennett H. Barrow and his wife Emily Barrow hang above the carved-cypress mantelpiece in the parlor at Highland.

Live Oak
Near Bains

Part of a 1796 Spanish land grant, Live Oak changed hands about fifteen times prior to 1928. In July of 1800 the land was sold by John O'Conner to Elijah Adams and his brother-in-law. It apparently was Adams who built the house in 1808. After Adams's death in 1816, Bennett Barrow of nearby Rosebank purchased the home and its 553 acres in 1824. For the next century it was owned by a succession of Barrow's descendants.

In 1928 Live Oak was bought by the William T. Le Sassier family, who operated a post office on the ground floor of the home. Upstairs, Mrs. Kate Le Sassier presided over a school for children of the area. The house remained in this family until the present owners took possession in 1975.

The magnificent structure has been authentically restored. The house, two full stories and an attic, has walls of brick, measuring one foot thick downstairs but narrowing slightly in the upper walls. Framing timbers are of rough-cut poplar, and much of the fine interior woodwork is also of poplar. Four heavy columns of rounded brick support the upper front gallery. Slender columns support the high-pitched roof. The simple floorplan includes four rooms with no dividing hallways on each story. The floors are connected by a tiny, hidden interior stairway, as well as by the two exterior ones.

During the 1930s a young girl fell in love with a watercolor of the house and purchased it on Royal Street in New Orleans. Throughout the years she grew to feel that the house, which she had seen only in her cherished painting, was somehow destined to be hers one day. In a happy quirk of fate, the young girl and her husband, Sue and Bert Turner of Baton Rouge, now own and cherish the fully restored Live Oak plantation house, which has been added to the National Historic Register.

Above the impressive dining room table at Live Oak hangs this unusual chandelier. The brick-lined mantelpiece stands next to the hidden interior stairway, which leads to the upper floor.

Note the unique chandelier above the game table in the comfortable sitting room at Live Oak.

The splendid full-tester, antique bed dominates this bedroom at Live Oak.

Detail of the dining room at Live Oak.

Upstairs view of the hidden stairway at Live Oak.

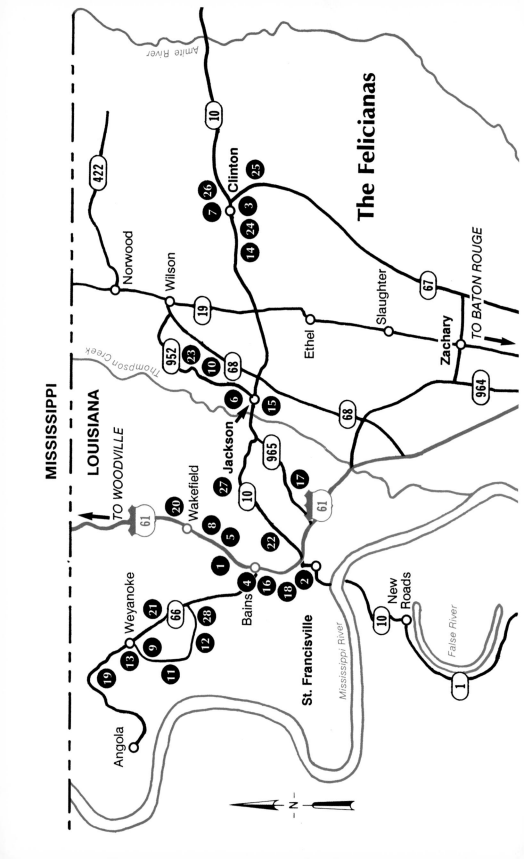

The Felicianas

51

Marston House
Clinton

Marston House was originally built as a bank in 1837. Spanning the width of the Greek Revival structure are six impressive plastered-brick Ionic columns which support a massive entablature. A palladian window adds to the elegance of the pediment.

This historic building was placed on the National Register of Historic Places in 1971.

Milbank
Jackson

Milbank was built in the 1830s as the banking house for the Clinton/ Port Hudson Railroad which traveled through Jackson. The establishment of the bank was instrumental in the growth of the town.

The building's imposing structure has a long, rich history, having housed some fifteen different businesses since its days as a bank. At one time it was the home of the first Jackson newspaper, the *Mirror*. In 1970, the Miller family purchased the building, began a major restoration, and made it their residence. The home has since changed ownership.

Because it was originally built for use as a bank, the interior floor plan differs from most homes of the antebellum period. The hallways, upper and lower, are located on one side of the house, and all the rooms are on the other side. The present owners have chosen to furnish the interior with antiques reflecting the 1800s.

Constructed of solid brick, Milbank's walls are two feet thick. Six impressive, plastered-brick Doric columns, front and rear, support the entablature.

This magnificent home is beautifully maintained by the present owners, Mr. Leroy Harvey and Mr. Thomas.

An antique clock of unique design stands on a pedestal in a corner of the Milbank parlor.

Against the Milbank parlor wall is a Dutch mahogany marquetry secretaire, dated 1840. It appears to be a chest of drawers, but the second drawer pulls out to convert it into a secretary. The Magnolia painting is by local artist Della Storms.

In the dining room at Milbank this spectacular solid-mahogany table commands attention. Surrounding it are unusually wide Irish Chippendale chairs. The silver candelabras were commissioned by Napoleon III in 1855 and bear the Napoleonic "N" and crown on the shields. Made by G. Stomes in Blackburn, England, the grandfather clock has a solid porcelain face.

Milbank's formal parlor is sometimes called the music room because of the musical instruments kept here. This view shows an antique square piano and a Spanish music cabinet made of cross-banded kingwood with gold Ormolu mounts on the front panels. The clock on top of the cabinet was made by Boque of Paris. In front of the American Victorian rosewood parlor set stands a black-lacquered opium chest, ca. 1860.

This antique rosewood piano at Milbank was made by Steinway & Son in 1857. The brass plate on the harp is inscribed, "Made by Broderys and Wilkinson in Haymarket, London."

One of the 80-pound Napoleonic candelabras at Milbank.

Although this room at Milbank is called the French Bedroom, the solid-brass bed is believed to have been owned by King Alphonso of Spain.

This bedroom at Milbank features a satin-lined half tester bed and armoire made of rosewood and walnut.

The Myrtles
St. Francisville

An elegant and mysterious mansion, the Myrtles was built on a Spanish land grant in 1796 by Gen. David Bradford, an exile from what was then the United States. Bradford had been a hero of the American Revolution, but he became involved in the Whiskey Rebellion of 1794 and had to flee to West Feliciana, which was Spanish territory at that time. He died in 1817, and the property passed to a succession of families.

Some of the finest examples of plaster friezework are found throughout the interior of the house. The Baccarat chandelier in the entrance hallway originally burned candles. The two parlors have ornate mirrors at opposite ends, twin Carrara marble mantels, chandeliers, and identical medallions. Wide galleries ornamented with elaborate ironwork grace the exterior of the one-and-a-half-story house. The high-pitched roof is broken by several dormer windows.

There allegedly have been sightings of ghosts at the Myrtles. Strange happenings remain unexplained: an unseen baby cries, the harmonium plays without human assistance, and the specter of a servant, who wore a *tignon* (turban) to hide the loss of an ear, wanders through the house.

The original pieces of art, the antique furnishings, and the beautifully restored house are all carefully maintained by the present owners.

Right: The mahogany staircase dominates the entrance hallway at the Myrtles.

Below: Happy hours are spent in the game room at the Myrtles. Note the antique game table. The two chairs with a swan motif were designed for Napoleon and Josephine.

This view of the parlor at the Myrtles calls attention to the beauty of the unique cornice-work and the Carrara marble mantelpiece.

In the Myrtles dining room, the late-eighteenth-century table and chairs are of satinwood.

Previous: Azaleas and Spanish moss add haunting beauty to the grounds of the Myrtles.

Above: The intricately carved medallion in the bedroom at the Myrtles, done in 1840, shows pineapples, grapes, and many different faces. The French beveled mirror above the marble mantelpiece has pierced carving at the top of the ornate frame.

Below: Twenty-carat gold trims the Louis XV bed.

Oakley
St. Francisville

This tall, airy house where John James Audubon stayed was built in 1799 by Ruffin Gray, who died before its completion. Lucy Alston, Gray's widow, inherited the Spanish land grant of 700 arpents and, through wise management, added 1,000 acres to the prosperous plantation.

Lucy later married James Pirrie and they had one daughter, Eliza, who became an impetuous young lady. The Pirries engaged Audubon for four months to tutor Eliza, allowing him half of each day to roam the woods, studying and painting birds. During this short period he produced thirty-two of his famous paintings.

The rooms at Oakley have been furnished in the style of the Federal period (1790-1830), duplicating their appearance when Audubon resided there.

The house reflects the expertise of colonials in dealing with a hot and humid climate. The shallow depth, the protective galleries, and the heavy jalousies all reflect the influence of the West Indies method of climate control. Simple and dignified, the building blends into its beautiful forest setting.

In 1973, Oakley was placed on the National Register of Historic Places. The house and grounds are now a part of the Audubon State Historic Site.

The Oakley greenhouse.

In this Oakley bedroom are a four-poster mahogany bed with a mosquito net draped over it and an antique wash basin.

The large, detached plantation kitchen, typical of the period, was reconstructed at Oakley on the old foundation around the original chimney.

The full-tester walnut bed in Eliza Pirrie's bedroom at Oakley stands next to the carved mantelpiece.

The plantation barn at Oakley displays numerous field tools and implements used to till the soil.

The parlor at Oakley.

Propinquity
St. Francisville

A trading post was established in 1790 by John Mills in the bustling town of Bayou Sara on the Mississippi River. He chose this location because the river traffic made the landing place lively with commerce, but it was to the high ground of nearby St. Francisville that he turned for a homesite. In 1809 Mills bought a lot in the town on historic Royal Street and built his dwelling. He enjoyed the house for a very short time, however, for he died in 1811.

William Center Wade, parish judge of Feliciana, rented the home for a time before purchasing it in 1816. He owned the property for only three years, but nearly a century and a half later it came into the possession of his great-grandson, Theodore H. Martin. Mr. and Mrs. Martin began thoughtful restoration of the interesting structure and named it Propinquity, meaning kinship or close proximity.

The current owners are Mike and Lea Reid Williams.

Originally, tapering brick walls fronted on the street. A doorway, now bricked up, gave access to an open gallery with exterior stairs. This gallery was enclosed and the wooden one added in 1826. The asymmetrical floor plan is unusual.

Propinquity was included in the National Register of Historic Places in 1973.

Top left: The dining room at Propinquity.

Top right: This bedroom at Propinquity features an impressive clover leaf poster bed from Nottoway Plantation, stained glass and a painting of a heron by local artist Samie Oneal.

Below: Empire mahogany pieces and a bust of George Washington grace the foyer at Propinquity.

Retreat Plantation House and St. Mary's Church
Near Weyanoke

Retreat Plantation House was built in the early 1820s by Capt. Clarence Mulford on a bluff overlooking Bayou Sara. The timeworn home stands amid old moss-draped oak trees. Poplar and bricks prepared on the plantation were used in its construction. Four stuccoed-brick Doric columns span the front of the house and support the steep hipped roof, which is broken by dormer windows.

Retreat is presently owned by C.B. and Mary Owen, the fifth generation of the Percy family to live in the house. A spectacular restoration was recently done with architect Frank Masson and builder W.J. Brown.

Nearby, in a dense woodland on the grounds of Retreat Plantation, stands St. Mary's Church *(See page 73)*. The quaint, Gothic-style church features crenellated tower parapets, lancet windows, and buttresses. An architectural treasure, it is listed on the National Register of Historic Places.

Although practically in ruins, the church is occasionally used as a beautiful spot for weddings. Concerned locals have formed an association to save St. Mary's Church. Restoration of the roof and windows is underway.

The dining room and parlor feature original Federal mantles. The Louis XV aubusson chairs in the parlor at Retreat were rescued from the 1960 fire at Greenwood.

What was just a few years ago an abandoned and dilapidated shell is now an elegant home appointed with period antiques and family heirlooms. The dining table at Retreat is made up of two sets of 1820s Campaign tables.

Designer Patrick Tandy helped with the recent restoration. The soft paint colors at Retreat are very close to the original.

The carved mahogany bedroom suite at Retreat was a wedding gift to Sarah and William Chaille Percy in 1865 and has remained in the house ever since.

Ruppert Kohlmaier created the fine reproduction of the Louisiana vernacular Campeche chair in the Retreat library. The Federal convex mirror dates to the early nineteenth century.

A statue of Diana, goddess of the hunt, in the gardens at Retreat.

St. Mary's Church, on the grounds of Retreat plantation.

Rosale
St. Francisville

West Feliciana Parish is often spoken of as English Louisiana, partially due to the background of the early settlers and partially due to the topography. One will find no better example of that characterization than Rosale.

Surrounded by over 100 magnificent live oak trees, the house is situated on a hill. Rolling hills and heavy forests in the distance give Rosale the appearance of being in the center of an English park.

On part of a large Spanish land grant made in 1795 to Alexander Stirling, his daughter Ann and her husband Andrew Skillman built a handsome red brick house in 1836. It had six columns front and back, two-and-a-half stories, and a full basement. A number of additional buildings were constructed near the manor. Two of these are still standing. One, a large two-story plantation schoolhouse, is incorporated in the present house. The other, a large and attractive Greek Revival summerhouse, stands nearby.

In 1845 Ann Skillman sold the plantation, then known as China Lodge, to Robert Hilliard Barrow, Jr., a descendant of the Pirries of Oakley and the Barrows of Highland. Robert and his wife, Mary Eliza, changed the name from China Lodge to Rosale. They lavished attention and money on Rosale, creating a grand manor and an elegant lifestyle. At that time members of the Barrow clan owned Highland, Greenwood, Rosebank, Live Oak, and Rosedown.

At the onset of the Civil War, Barrow raised and outfitted a company of volunteers, the Rosale Guards. In time he became commander of the Eleventh Louisiana Infantry and commanded that unit at the Battle of Shiloh.

The Civil War and Reconstruction brought an end to the golden era of the planter class. Most of the great houses survived, although ownership changed often, as did the lifestyles of the occupants.

Throughout the years, fire was a constant threat to plantation homes. Indeed, Rosale burned to the ground in 1888. The 1835 two-story schoolhouse, complete with two chimneys, thick plaster walls, heart-of-pine flooring, and huge poplar sills, was moved to the site of the original house. To this intact core was added a broader center hallway and several additional rooms, plus a surrounding gallery.

The present owners of Rosale, Lynda and Peter Truitt, are restoring the house to its original grandeur.

Left: The well house at Rosale.
Right: This view of the original stairway at Rosale shows the attractive design of the rails.

The gallery at Rosale looks out to the well house.

Rosale's original slave cabins date to well before the Civil War. Slave cabins at Oakley Plantation State Historic Site were donated by the owners of Rosale.

Rosebank
Near Bains

While the exact date of construction is unknown, Rosebank exhibits definite evidence of early Spanish influence, particularly in its exterior staircases and the straight, unbroken line of its cedar-shake roof. The land was part of a 1790s Spanish land grant held by an Irishman, John O'Conner, who served as *alcade* of the district during the last years of Spanish rule. O'Conner is said to have operated an inn on the lower floor of the house.

In 1818 the house was purchased by Bennett Barrow, brother of Bartholomew Barrow of Afton Villa. Bennett Barrow became a cotton planter and political leader, representing the parish in the Louisiana Legislature in 1827.

Bennett's youngest son, Robert James Barrow, who had been only seven months of age when the family came to Louisiana, inherited Rosebank at age sixteen. It was Robert's wife who gave Rosebank its name and planted the profusion of old-fashioned bulbs which brighten its lawn in early spring with colorful blooms.

Misfortune plagued Robert Barrow's life. His first four children died in infancy, and he suffered numerous financial setbacks. The Civil War brought still another reversal when he was taken prisoner by Union soldiers.

The lower floor has eighteen-inch-thick walls of *bousillage*, a mixture of mud, moss, and deer hair. The bricks used in the exterior walls and the flooring of the ground level were made on the plantation. The upper levels contain the main living quarters and are solidly constructed of cypress and blue poplar. Wooden pegs join the mortised beams and joists. Four Doric columns support the upper-floor gallery, and slender iron colonnettes support the roof.

A spectacular restoration has been completed by the present owners, Beverly and David Walker.

Left: Beverly Walker's collection of cut-glass decanters and sterling-silver mint julep cups are displayed under the stairs at Rosebank.

Below: The dining room at Rosebank, with brick flooring and bold paint colors original to the house. The Louis XVI chairs are covered in cerulean blue leather.

The ceiling of the wine room at Rosebank is covered in wicker baskets.

The luxurious parlor at Rosebank features an Empire crystal chandelier matching the one in the dining room one floor below, sofas covered in Scalamandre velvet and silk, and a baby grand piano.

Rosedown
St. Francisville

Daniel Turnbull, a wealthy planter, made an entry in his journal on November 3, 1834, which signaled the beginning of work to create Rosedown. Construction of the home was completed in 1835.

He and his wife, Martha Barrow Turnbull, shortly before had returned from their wedding trip to Europe where they had purchased magnificent furnishings for the mansion they intended to build. At Versailles and in the gardens of Italy Martha saw avenues of trees, statuary, formal parterres, and garden ornaments in the French style of the seventeenth century. Plans for her garden began to form in her mind, and on her return her plans were carried out.

Today the interior of Rosedown is filled with beautiful antiques, reflecting the elegant lifestyle of the antebellum years.

Impressive Doric columns extend across the two-story central section of the house. Wooden balustrades of classic design encircle both upper and lower galleries. Cypress and cedar used in building this spectacular mansion came from a swamp woodland on the property and was processed at the plantation's sawmill. One-story plastered-brick wings, each with a portico and columns, were built on either side of the house.

Descendants of the Turnbulls lived in the home until 1956 when the late Catherine Fondren Underwood of Houston, Texas, bought and restored Rosedown to its original grandeur.

The Carrara marble mantelpiece dominates the parlor at Rosedown. The hand-and-arm tiebacks holding the window draperies are unique.

The original furnishings purchased by the Turnbulls for Rosedown included this Regency mahogany dining table, Phyfe chairs, and a French Empire serving table with console marble top. On one side of the cotton covering of the punkah are flowers and cotton blossoms.

While in Paris, Martha and Daniel Turnbull purchased this scenic wallpaper for Rosedown. Designed by Joseph Dufour, a celebrated craftsman, it enhances the breathtaking foyer.

The Turnbulls' daughter Sarah and her husband, James Bowman from neighboring Oakley Plantation, used the Floral Bedroom at Rosedown as their master bedroom. The mahogany, half-tester bed is original to the house and was purchased from Prudent Mallard in the late 1850s or early 1860s.

Other original pieces in the Floral Bedroom at Rosedown include a marble top washstand and an Empire day bed with horsehair mattress.

In springtime the gazebo at Rosedown is surrounded by colorful azaleas.

The quiet beauty of the scene in the vast gardens of Rosedown.

The Shades
Near Gurley

Built of cypress hewn on the plantation, and hand-fashioned bricks, the Shades plantation house was completed in 1808 by Alexander Scott, who had heard intriguing tales of fortunes being made in the lush region of Louisiana. He had originally settled in Black Mingo, South Carolina, and came to Louisiana with his long rifle, which he affectionately called "Old Black Mingo" in tribute to his former home.

With Old Black Mingo in the crook of his elbow and his dog at his heels, Alexander roamed the woodlands hunting game for his dinner table while he lived in a cabin and watched the walls of his beautiful new home rise.

After having enjoyed the comfort and peace of the Shades for nearly fifty years, Alexander died in the 1840s. Upon his death, the home was inherited by his son, Maj. E. A. Scott, who with his brother, Capt. Gus Scott, served with distinction in the First Louisiana Cavalry during the Civil War. Family records indicate that the major's son, Alexander Scott II, who had inherited some of his grandfather's mettle, ran away from home at the age of fifteen to join the Confederate forces.

The daughter of Alexander Scott II, Eva Scott, was a jolly, well-loved lady who had been born in one of the upstairs bedrooms in 1877. It was during Miss Eva's residency that the home became known as "the house of bells" because of

her collection of more than 1,000 bells amassed over the years. They are displayed in the house today.

The rectangular structure consists of two stories. It has a steep, double-pitched roof, the lower level of which is supported by massive Doric columns.

The Shades is now owned by Jacqueline Berger Westerfield, a descendant of Alexander Scott. Thus, the Shades remains in the original family's possession.

A magnificent Prudent Mallard cabinet houses the bell collection at the Shades.

An ornate, mahogany bedroom set with carved faces at the Shades has been in the family for many generations.

More of Eva Scott's bell collection is on display on one of the Shades' many fireplace mantels. Framed above is a print of the old Silliman Institute.

The massive four-poster bed in this bedroom at the Shades is in early Louisiana style.

86

Silliman Institute
Clinton

Under the influence and leadership of William Silliman, ten public-spirited citizens of East Feliciana Parish, realizing the value of education for young women, formed a corporation in May 1852 and called it Silliman Female Collegiate Institute. A site for the college was obtained in a suburb of Clinton and construction was begun.

In the first year of operation, 1852-53, ninety-six students enrolled. When the Civil War broke out in 1861, the institute's doors were closed and remained so throughout the conflict. Silliman was used as a hospital for wounded soldiers during the Battle of Clinton.

After the Civil War, most of the corporation stockholders were so impoverished that they transferred their interests to William Silliman, the only one possessing the means, and the courage, to proceed. Silliman then transferred the grounds, buildings, and an endowment fund of twenty thousand dollars to the Louisiana Presbytery, the lower court of the Presbyterian Church. The conditions of the donation were that the Presbytery, through its agents and trustees in perpetual succession, would conduct the institution as a college for young ladies, free from all sectarian tenets and religious dogmas. The buildings at the college remained the same until 1894 when a fifty-by-one-hundred-foot structure was added.

Eighteen immense Doric columns span the façade of the three connected, yet dissimilar, structures. Magnificent oak, beech, and magnolia trees shade the campus.

Stonehenge
Clinton

High on a hill in a grove of magnificent old trees, Stonehenge stands in stately splendor. Construction took place in 1837 by Judge Lafayette Saunders, who later built the present Clinton courthouse in 1841. He and his family lived in the home for only a brief time. After his young daughter plunged to her death through an open window on the second floor, the Saunders family abandoned the new mansion.

Shortly after the tragedy, Judge John McVea purchased the property. Upon his death in 1876 the estate was inherited by his daughter, Imogen, and her husband, Col. John Stone. The new owners named the home Stonehenge.

The palatial house has upper and lower galleries which span its width. Six imposing, fluted Doric columns support the upper gallery and exquisite, lacy iron filigree supports the sloping roof. The walls are of brick, twelve inches thick.

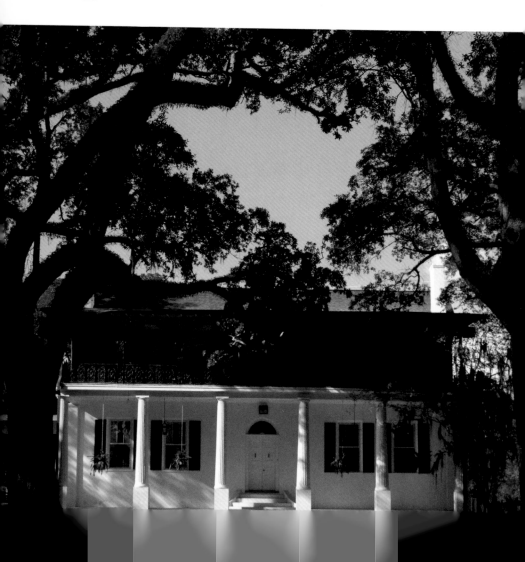

Wall House
Clinton

A quaint cottage called the Wall House stands on a quiet street in the center of Clinton. The original portion of the house was constructed in the late 1830s by the Reverend Isaac Wall, Sr., a Methodist minister originally from New York. His son, Isaac Wall, Jr., enlarged the home in an 1895 remodeling.

Wall House is a story-and-a-half frame house with Queen Anne Revival and Italianate features. It was originally one room deep and three rooms wide. The age of this part of the house is indicated by its wide floorboards and its pit sawed (or water mill sawed) joists. In the late 1800s a front and a side wing were added. The date of these sections of the house is corroborated by the fact that the floorboards are narrow and the joists are circular sawed. The floor plan was reworked at that time to include a central hall. The front parlor received a turret with a faceted conical roof.

Architecturally significant, the Wall House is a landmark in Clinton's heritage of late-nineteenth-century residences.

The National Register of Historic Places added the Wall House to its list on May 31, 1984.

Wildwood

Near St. Francisville

In 1915 Wildwood, originally called Arrowhead, was built by architect Robert S. Soulé for his brother, Albert Lee Soulé, a highly respected educator from New Orleans. Soulé's father had founded Soulé Commercial College in New Orleans in 1856, and the Feliciana home provided the family needed respite on weekends from the responsibilities of running the institute.

Designed as a showcase of the most progressive ideas of the day, the home featured central heating, closets for each bedroom, an intercom system, an electric bell for maid service, tile-lined chimneys, and three bathrooms, excluding the one in the basement for the hired help. A laundry chute was built on the second floor, extending to the basement where washing vats were installed. The house also had a butler's pantry and a solarium.

The elder Soulé took a great interest in the home's lawns and planted many camellias which continue to thrive today. He also supervised the planting of the rows of crepe myrtle trees.

In 1958 the magnificent home was sold to the Conrad P. McVea family, and history seemingly repeated itself. The McVeas were both educators, the husband a longtime associate with the State Department of Education and the wife the first-grade teacher for a generation of school children. The McVeas renamed the home Wildwood after their ancestral property near Port Hudson. The mansion is maintained beautifully by Tom and Toni McVea as their private home.

Left: Original crystal chandelier and stained glass at Wildwood.

Bottom: Wildwood is exquisitely furnished with Empire and Victorian antiques.

Much of the bedroom furniture at Wildwood has belonged to the McVea family for generations.

Woodland
St. Francisville

On a lovely, green hillside near Highland Plantation is a house called Woodland with an amazing and complex story. The current owners, Cammie and David Norwood, first cousin to the Highland Norwoods, fell in love with the overgrown house in ruins along I-49 in St. Landry Parish. When they heard that the owner planned to demolish the crumbling Greek Revival gem, they asked if they could have it. It took a year to prepare the house for the move about forty miles from its original location to land adjacent to Highland Plantation near St. Francisville. It took another year to put it back together.

Sugar baron Amos Webb built Woodland for his son, Dr. Louis Archibald Webb, when he graduated from medical school at the University of Virginia in 1847. Amos Webb had many ties to St. Francisville. He was the first U.S. Postmaster of St. Francisville and lived in the Camilla Leake Barrow House soon after it was built in 1809.

During the Civil War, Woodland served as a hospital for Confederate soldiers. It even sustained damage from Union artillery fire.

The thirty-seven-mile relocation required hundreds of miles of travel on back roads. To move the delicate structure, the first and third floors, as well as the second-floor center hall, were disassembled. The double parlors and twelve-foot-deep front and back porches were moved in one piece. Much of the millwork was

intact, so all pieces of flooring, doors, cornices, mantles, shutters, porch railing, and other items were numbered and put back into place like a giant puzzle.

In the parlor, the Norwoods placed a portrait of William Barrow Ratliff, which they fortuitously bought for its historical value. But Ratliff's presence here is a perfect symbol of the tightly woven connections between almost all the great plantations of South Louisiana. William was the grandson of Bartholomew Barrow who built the first Barrow house, Locust Grove or Locust Ridge, now known as Highland, and established Afton Villa, where this book begins. The current owner of Woodland, David Norwood, descends from the same Barrow bloodline, and Woodland stands on land that was originally part of Greenwood Plantation, built by William Ruffin Barrow, son of Bartholomew Barrow. Multiple branches of the Barrow family built and still own most of the plantation homes in the area.

Left: In the sunny parlor at Woodland, above the original Cyprus mantle is a portrait of William Barrow Ratliff.

Right: Woodland's upper hallway with its graceful arches.

Family heirlooms fill the master bedroom at Woodland. The headboard of this massive bed is topped by a removable rolling pin that the servants would use to smooth the lumpy, moss-filled mattresses and feather beds.

On the dining room mantle at Woodland are blackamoor candle holders and a glass fly catcher. To help control the flies at the dinner table with all the windows open, fly catchers were filled with a bit of sugar water. Flies would enter the vessel and could not find their way out.